DEVELOPING COMPREHENSION

Red Book

Alan Lynskey

Margaret Stillie

STANLEY
THORNES

Red - orange -
gm - blue

Contents

Introduction

Developing Comprehension is an attempt to clarify and to develop the many skills involved in the real comprehension of language.

The Barret taxonomy, on which the series is based, presents five main categories of comprehension.

1 Literal comprehension: answering questions by direct reference to the text. These answers are usually explicitly stated in the passage.

2 Reorganisational comprehension: classifying, collecting and organising information explicitly stated in the passage. The information may be collected from more than one source.

3 Inferential comprehension: detecting information implied in a passage. This demands thinking and deduction beyond what appears in the passage.

4 Evaluative comprehension: interpreting and evaluating the writer's assumptions or intentions, often by comparison with the reader's own experiences or opinions.

5 Appreciative comprehension: responding to a passage with enjoyment, and with an awareness of its language usage and emotion.

Obviously these skills are not clear cut and separate. There is a considerable overlap between categories. Certainly the higher-level skills − the ability to appreciate and evaluate written material − require the child to exercise literal and re-organisational skills in order to reach decisions.

Techniques
Developing Comprehension uses a variety of techniques to develop reading skills:

Prediction
Predictions are vital to the reader's active involvement in what he or she is reading. In the exercises we ask "What do you think happens next?" In the classroom children should be asked to discuss their predictions and the evidence which supports them. Teachers can give more practice in prediction by breaking a passage into sections and asking "Where do you think this is happening?" "What will so-and-so do next?" "What will happen then?". When the next section is read, the children can evaluate and revise their predictions in the light of what they have learnt.

Cloze texts
These are passages with words omitted, which children are asked to supply. Often there is no right or wrong answer. The child is asked to supply the best word he or she can think of which contributes to the meaning and the feeling of the passage. If the chosen word can be justified, then it can be judged as right. Sometimes the missing word will be determined by the structure of the

4

sentence, and there will be little argument. But in every case, discussion of alternatives and reasons for choices is vital to the learning process.

Sequencing and ordering

The child is asked to place events in order or sequence. Technically, he or she will need to be able to pick up indicator clues (next, but, etc.) which relate one paragraph to another, and then comprehend the underlying pattern of a passage — to understand across whole paragraphs the development of events. These passages are especially valuable when used in small group discussion. Some whole-class oral work will complete the lesson.

Evaluation

The teacher needs to have clear purposes of evaluation. *Developing Comprehension* is designed to evaluate and improve children's ability to read and fully comprehend. Answers, therefore, should be evaluated initially by the way they display the child's understanding and appreciation of what he or she has read. Classroom discussions should begin with meaning, before looking at how to record that meaning in written English.

The work produced, written or oral, indicates to the teacher the strengths and weaknesses of each child. Programmes of work can be developed to cater for the weaknesses of individuals or groups of children.

The evaluation of responses to cloze texts and prediction and sequencing exercises will be oral as comparisons are made and reasons put forward as to why one choice is better or worse than another. Discussion sessions are crucial in helping children to see what they have missed in their reading, and they encourage purposeful re-reading, which is a vital higher-level skill.

Marking and assessment

The responses or answers a child makes are a starting point for teaching, not a final assessment. Even a totally inappropriate answer will provide a basis on which to work.

The level of difficulty of a passage in relation to a child's reading level must be taken into account in any assessment. No child can be expected to make an evaluation or appreciation of a passage he or she can read only with difficulty. But teacher expectation is a significant factor in pupils' attainment and should not be pitched too low.

We have chosen passages of high literary merit, including the best writers of contemporary children's fiction. We hope that children will be encouraged to read more of the work of the writers they have enjoyed.

ALAN LYNSKEY
MARGARET STILLIE

Sam's ghost

Sam and Dave are Cubs.

When they go to Cubs they go down an alley by the churchyard. The churchyard is full of old graves.

In summer it's all right, but in winter they don't like it
5 very much.

In winter the alley is very creepy. There is just one lamp halfway down. The rest is dark.

One dark night after Cubs, Dave said, "Look!" He stood still and pointed his finger. "Look, Sam, there's a
10 ghost!"

Sam looked and he saw it.

It was all white and wavy, by a big gravestone!

Sam and Dave ran like mad.

Next day at school, Dave said, "Let's go and look
15 tonight, Sam. Let's see if the ghost is still there."

Sam didn't want to much, but he said, "OK."

So that night they went down the alley again, and when they got to the same place as before, there was the ghost, all white and wavy. It looked very spooky.
20 Sam wanted to run, but Dave said, "No, let's go and look at it. Let's go into the churchyard and take a good look."

Sam said he didn't want to, so Dave said he'd look on his own. Dave was very brave.
25 When Dave said he'd go on his own, Sam was brave too. He said he'd go as well.

So they went down the alley and by the scout-hut and into the churchyard, and round the side of the church where the big grave was.

Here's Sam
Dorothy Edwards

1 What did the ghost look like?
2 What were the boys doing when they first saw the ghost?
3 What did the boys do when they first saw it?
4 How do Sam and David get to Cubs?
5 What plan do the boys make at school?
6 How was the alley different in winter than in summer? What causes this difference?
7 Why didn't Sam want to go back to the churchyard?
8 How can you tell that Sam and David were good friends?
9 Which boy behaves most like you would do?
10 What do you think happens in the story next? Is there really a ghost?
11 Here are three sentences from the passage with the words mixed up. Write out each sentence putting the words in the correct order.

Cubs   and   Sam   are   David.
looked   he   Sam   and   it   saw.
he'd   said   go   as   well   he.

The spell

Ursula loves bears so much that her greatest wish is to become a bear.

Every day for a week Ursula ate nothing but porridge and honey and currant buns. Every day for a week she looked in the mirror as soon as she woke up. But all she saw was the same pink face and brown curls and
5 blue eyes.
On Saturday she went to the library. In the library she found a book about magic spells. On page one hundred and sixty-three it said, "How a little girl can turn into a bear."
10 Ursula closed her eyes tight. Then she opened them and looked again. It was true. That's just what it said on page one hundred and sixty-three. "How a little girl can turn into a bear."
Ursula asked the librarian for a piece of paper and a
15 pencil. She copied down the spell.
"Two tablespoons porridge, one tablespoon honey, one large currant bun. Stir porridge and honey together and make into a sandwich with currant bun. Recite these magic words while eating bun. *I'm a bear,*
20 *I'm a bear, I'm a bear, I'm a bear, I'm a bear, I'm a bear.* To change back into a little girl again . . ."
But Ursula did not bother to read the rest. She ran all the way home, clutching her piece of paper tightly in her hand. She had been eating all the right things, but
25 they hadn't worked without the magic words. Now she knew what to do.

Ursula Bear
Sheila Lavelle

8

1 What did Ursula eat to try to change into a bear? Why do you think she chose those things?
2 Write down everything she needed to make the spell work.
3 What did Ursula do as soon as she woke up? Why did she do that?
4 What did Ursula look like?
5 Why did she "close her eyes tight"?
6 What did she have to do while eating, to make the spell work?
7 How do you think Ursula felt when she found this spell?
8 Why did she not copy out the second part of the spell?
9 How would you like to eat nothing but porridge, honey and currant buns for a week?
10 What do you think the part of the spell to turn Ursula back into a girl might have been?

Pandas

Far away, in the mountains of China, there lives a special kind of animal. It is called a giant panda. A full-grown giant panda is as big as a black bear. It is about six feet long from its head to its tail. Giant pandas are
5 furry and fat. They look like great big teddy bears, only they are not brown like teddy bears. They are black and white.

Their legs are black. Their shoulders are black. Their ears are black, and the fur around their black eyes is
10 black too. Everywhere else their fur is white. Pandas have white faces and white middles and short white tails.

In the mountains where the pandas live, it is cold and damp. Snow covers the ground until May or June, and
15 the summers are rainy and wet. All the year round, bamboo plants grow tall and thick. Many years ago, hunters used to go to the mountains to shoot the pandas. Then the Chinese government said that nobody could shoot pandas any more. Nowadays
20 Chinese people sometimes climb the high mountains to look for a baby panda. When they find one, they carry it carefully down the mountains and take it to a zoo.

A Book about Pandas
R. B. Gross

1 In which country do pandas live?
2 Which toy do pandas look like?
3 How big is a full grown panda?
4 Which parts of the panda are black?
5 What is the weather like in the mountains where the pandas live?
6 Why do you think the panda needs thick fur?
7 Which plant do you think the panda likes to eat?
8 Why do you think the pandas were hunted?
9 Do you think baby pandas should be kept in zoos? Why do you think so?
10 Why do you think the Chinese Government stopped hunters from shooting pandas?
11 What word in the passage makes you think the Chinese look after their pandas?
12 Read the words in this list, and write out the words which you think fit the panda.

fierce   free   plump   playful
angry   cuddly   kind

Mike's bike

One day a big truck drove up to the rubbish dump. It stopped and two men got out. They went to the back of the truck and took out wheelbarrows and shovels.

Mike watched as the men shovelled and shovelled.
5   They moved paperbags and old boots. They moved tin cans and old rags. They even moved the rusty old car. All the time the rubbish dump was getting smaller and smaller.

When the truck was full the men put down their
10   shovels and their wheelbarrows. They got into the truck and drove it away. Mike stared and stared, and his eyes grew bigger and bigger. He didn't see the birds perched on the wheels because they had flown away. He didn't see the mouse who lived under the saddle because it
15   had run away. But he did see the rusty old bike in the middle of the rubbish dump.

Mike ran all the way to the tall block of flats where he lived with his mother and father. He told them about the bike. Then Mike and his father ran all the way back
20   to the rubbish dump. The men with the truck were just moving the bike.

"Please may we have the bike?" asked Mike's father.

"Yes," said the men, and gave it to Mike.

Mike and his father took the bike back to their flat.
25   "It needs a good clean and a polish," said Mike's mother.

Mike's Bike
Marjorie Darke

12

1 Who got out of the big truck?
2 What was Mike most interested in?
3 Where did Mike live?
4 What were the men doing?
5 What did the men do to clear the rubbish dump? Write down everything the passage tells you.
6 Why did the rubbish dump get smaller and smaller?
7 Why did Mike's eyes get bigger and bigger?
8 Why did Mike run back to the flats?
9 Why did Mike and his father run all the way to the rubbish dump?
10 Do you think Mike knew the bike was in the dump? Why?
11 What else might they have to do to the bike as well as clean it?
12 Read what Mike's mother said. What sort of person do you think she is?

Making sense

Here are eight lines of a poem. They are written in pairs but not in the right order. Read them all first.

Then talk about the order you think they should be in. Write down the letters in the order you think the pairs should be. Do you agree with your friends?

A A feather bed and a wooden leg,
And a pair of calico breeches.

B A coffee pot without a spout,
A mug without a handle,

C A baccy box without a lid
And half a farthing candle.

D My Aunt she died a month ago
And left me all her riches,

Now try the same with these eight lines.

A For as he sleeps upon the Nile
He thinner gets and thinner,

B Ignore the welcome in his smile
Be careful not to stroke him.

C If you should meet a crocodile,
Don't take a stick and poke him

D And when'er you meet a crocodile
He's ready for his dinner.

How to be a giant

The paragraphs below are not in the right order.
   Read them all first then talk about the order you think they should be in.
   Write down the letters in the order you think they should be.
   Talk about your order with your friends.

A The smaller one of you sits on the other's shoulders.

B The top half gets into the hat and coat. The bottom half does up the buttons. Leave a gap to peer through as you stride around.

C The taller one of you wears trousers and puts the rubber gloves on your feet — large orange gloves look best.

D You will need a friend, a hat, a long coat, a pair of trousers and maybe a pair of rubber gloves. Your friend should be much taller or smaller than you are.

E Practise walking around until you are quite steady.

Body Tricks
Penguin Books

Meeting Sunday

Ben and Kathy want a dog of their own, but they live in a flat in a big city and dogs aren't allowed. One Sunday they go with their big sister to the Park and a big shaggy dog makes friends with them.

Now other children were coming, some from the play-park, some just arriving through the gates. "What is it?" "Is it yours?"

To the first question, Ben said, with secret pride, "It's
5   an Old English Sheepdog, of course, a pedigree one." He had seen a photograph in a library book. To the second he said nothing, merely sat loftily, not hearing, and left everyone to decide for himself.

After a little while, when the crowd was quite big, he
10 got to his feet and said, "Come on." The dog rose and came with him.

The crowd parted hastily, to make way. Some children ran quite a distance and then, seeing nobody had been eaten, came running back .

15 Kathy stood alone, watching, then quietly skipped towards them and took her place on the other side of the dog. So they walked across the grass, the two of them, as if the dog were their own.

Then Kathy took out her ball and threw it. It
20 bounced, and the dog seemed to bounce with it. They bounced and bounced, the dog and the ball, and Ben and Kathy shrieked with laughter, and rolled on the grass. The dog ran over and sat on Ben. Ben spluttered, and pushed him off, and the dog ran round
25 and round a tree.

"How can he see without eyes?" said Kathy.

"Of course he has eyes," said Ben scornfully, "His hair grows over them, that's all."

"I don't like him to be like that," said Kathy. "He'll
30 bump into something and frighten himself." She took a clip from her hair, and walked over to the dog, and he sat down quietly while she fastened his hair back. "There, that's better," she said.

Then they raced in and out of the trees, dodging,
35 playing hide-and-seek, bumping into one another, shrieking and squealing. The dog bumped into no one; he could dodge better than either of them.

My Dog Sunday
Leila Berg

1 How did Ben know the dog is an Old English Sheepdog?

2 Why do the children who ran away from the dog come back?

3 Why does Kathy think the dog has no eyes?

4 Write about the games Ben and Kathy play with the dog.

5 Why does Ben answer the first question he is asked but not the second?

6 What does Kathy do for the dog?

7 How do you think the children feel when they walk across the grass with the big dog between them?

8 Why are people not allowed to keep big dogs in city flats?

9 Why do you think Ben and Kathy laugh and roll on the grass?

10 Look at the title of the story. The children have called the dog Sunday. Why did they choose that name?

17

My cat

My cat's name is Whiskers. He is a black and white cat. He has very long whiskers and a small face. His ears are pointed and he has big green eyes and is quite large. He is fluffy and soft to the touch and nice to
5 stroke.

At night he sleeps on our beds and when it is cold he comes right up to me to keep warm. After breakfast he goes out into the garden for the day. In the winter he goes to a sheltered place then curls up in the sun to
10 keep warm, out of the cold wind.

In the summer when the sun is very hot he stretches out at full length with his white tummy showing in the shade at the edge of the lawn. In the garden he spends his time watching the birds feeding and the little field
15 mice in the shrubbery. He chases grasshoppers and lizards and dances after butterflies. When Mummy works in the garden he comes and sits in her shadow.

Sometimes he hides behind bushes and when we come past he jumps out at us and we chase him all over
20 the lawn. Sometimes he comes in with a bird and goes under the bed and if we come too close he growls. After he has eaten the bird he leaves lots and lots of feathers under the bed and Mummy gets up to come and sweep it away and she gets so cross.

25 When we go out he is our watch cat. He sits on the top of the roof and waits till we come back. As we come down the drive we can see his big green eyes looking back at us. When Mummy unlocks the door he is the first to go in meowing all the way to the kitchen

30 refrigerator for his food, fresh mincemeat. Whenever we open the refrigerator door he is always there.

Sarah Nesbitt (aged 8)

1 What colour is Whiskers's tummy?
2 How does he spend his time in the garden?
3 Where does he wait when they go out?
4 How does he keep warm on cold nights?
5 How does he keep cool when watching Mummy work in the garden?
6 Read the passage again to notice everything it tells you about what Whiskers looks like. Write a description of Whiskers in your own words.
7 Why is Mummy cross when he takes birds under the bed?
8 Why does he growl when people get too close when he is eating the bird?
9 Why do you think Sarah called her cat Whiskers? What would you call a cat?
10 Why is he always there when the refrigerator door opens?
11 Why does he jump out from behind the bushes?

The tenth good thing about Barney

My cat Barney died last Friday
I was very sad.

I cried, and I didn't watch television.
I cried, and I didn't eat my chicken or even
5 the chocolate pudding.
I went to bed, and I cried.

My mother sat down on my bed, and she
gave me a hug.
She said we could have a funeral for
10 Barney in the morning.
She said I should think of ten good things
about Barney so I
could tell them at the funeral.

I thought, and I thought, and I thought of
15 good things about Barney.
I thought of nine good things.
Then I fell asleep.

In the morning my mother wrapped
Barney in a yellow scarf.
20 My father buried Barney in the ground by a
tree in the garden.
Annie, my friend from next door, came
over with flowers.
And I told good things about Barney.

25 Barney was brave, I said.
And smart and funny and clean.

Also cuddly and handsome, and he only
once ate a bird.
It was sweet, I said, to hear him purr in my ear.
30 And sometimes he slept on my tummy and
kept it warm.

Those are all good things, said my mother,
but I just count nine.
I said I would try to think of another one later.

The Tenth Good Thing About Barney
Judith Viorst

1 Who was Barney?
2 How many good things had the child to think of?
3 On which day of the week was Barney buried?
4 Write down what the child did and didn't do, the day Barney died.
5 The child's mother does three things to try and make the child feel better. What are they?
6 At the funeral, mother, father and Annie each do something for Barney. Write down what they did.
7 Why did the child not think of the tenth good thing?
8 Look at the list of good things the child remembers about Barney — choose the two you think are the nicest. Write them down.
9 Think about cats you have known and the things they do. Make up your own tenth thing which might fit Barney.
10 Which of these words do you think fits the child's mother? Write them down.

     kind   thoughtful   cross   busy
       understanding   helpful

Danny Fox and the fish man

Danny Fox is a very tricky animal. Here we read how he tricks the fish man and gets his dinner.

When the driver saw Danny lying stretched in the middle of the road, he stopped his cart and said, "That's funny. That's the fox that was stealing my fish. That's the fox I hit with my whip. I thought I had only
5 touched the tip of his tail, but now I see I must have hurt him badly. He must have run away from me ahead of my cart. And now he is dead."

He got down from his cart and stooped to look at Danny.

10 "What a beautiful red coat he's got," the driver said, "and what beautiful, thick red trousers. What a beautiful long bushy tail, with a beautiful white tip. What a beautiful long smooth nose with a beautiful black tip. I'll take him home with me, I think, and skin
15 him and sell his fur."

So he picked up Danny Fox and threw him on to the cart on top of the boxes of fish. The cart went on.

Danny opened one eye and saw the driver's back was turned to him. Then very quietly, he slid the tip of
20 his tail underneath a fish and flicked it on to the road. He lay quite still and threw another fish out with his tail, then another and another, till all down the road behind the cart there was a long, long line of fish stretching into the distance. And the driver never looked round
25 because he thought Danny was dead.

At the next corner, Danny jumped off the cart and ran back down the road. When the cart was out of sight, he started to pick the fish up.

Danny Fox
D. Thompson

1 Why did the driver think that Danny was dead?
2 What had the driver done to Danny?
3 Why did the driver take him home?
4 Where does the driver first see Danny Fox?
5 In your own words, tell how Danny got the fish out of the cart.
6 Write down *all* that the driver thought when he stopped his cart.
7 From what the driver says (line 10), write a description of Danny.
8 How do you think Danny felt as he ran home with the fish?
9 Do you think he had planned to be thrown in the cart? Why?
10 Why do you think he jumped off the cart at a corner?
11 Read the words in this list and then write out the ones you think fit Danny Fox.

timid   cunning   slow   quick-witted
    clever   angry   lazy

Witches' spells

The sky is dark, the stars are bright,
The moon is shining too
Inside a cave the witches meet
To mix their favourite brew.

5 They light a fire, and when it flames
They fetch a big black pot;
They fill it up with lizards' blood,
Then wait till it's hot.

Each one has brought a magic charm
10 To put into the stew,
A spider's web, a fairy's wing,
A beetle's leg, or two.

They take a stick, and bending low
They stir the mixture round.
15 They rub their fingers, old and cramped
And stamp upon the ground.

Their wizened faces grin with glee,
As round the pot they prance,
Their sharp eyes glisten in the dark,
20 Their cloaks swirl as they dance.

They drink, and then into the sky,
On broomsticks, swift and light,
They cackle hoarsely as they fly,
And soon are out of sight.

A. Nightingale

1 Where do the witches meet?
2 What do the witches put in the pot first?
3 What charms do the witches put into the pot?
4 What do the witches do after they stir the mixture?
5 Why do the witches meet?
6 What do the witches look like as they dance round the pot?
7 What do you think the witches want the charms for?
8 Why do the witches rub their fingers?
9 Read the last verse of the poem, and write out the line which tells you the witches are pleased with their night's work.
10 Where do you think the witches might be flying to?
11 Find words in the passage with these meanings.

laugh	c . . . .
dry and wrinkled	w . . . .
shine	g . . . .
to dance in a lively way	p . . . .
happiness	g . . . .

The earth and the moon

The higher up you go the more of the earth you can see. From an aeroplane you can see the countryside below. If we go into space we see more and more of the earth. One reason why people and machines are
5 sent out into space is to look at the earth and learn more about it. Another reason is to find out more about the stars, planets and other bodies around us.

The moon is the nearest body to the earth. It is smaller than the earth and has no air or water. This is
10 one reason why plants cannot grow on the moon.

The moon travels all the way round the earth, taking a little more than 27 days to complete its orbit. The same side of the moon always faces the earth. It does not spin round like the earth.

15 The moon has no light of its own. It shines back the light of the sun. When the sun is shining on the side of the moon that faces us it looks like a great round ball. This is a full moon. At times we cannot see the moon because the sun is shining on the side facing away from
20 us. Sometimes we see a thin curved part of the moon, called a crescent moon. Then the sun is shining mostly on the side of the moon that faces away from us but just beginning to shine on the part we can see. This part grows until it becomes a full moon.

1 Why do plants not grow on the moon?
2 Which is the nearest body to earth?
3 How does the moon get its light?
4 How long does it take the moon to travel round the earth?
5 What does the full moon look like?
6 What two reasons are there for space travel?
7 Where is the sun shining when we have (a) a full moon (b) a crescent moon?
8 The passage tells you some ways in which the moon is different from the earth. Name two of them.
9 Choose the right answer:

Sometimes we can't see the moon because
(a) it is too far away;
(b) clouds are covering the sun;
(c) the sun is shining on a part we can't see.

Plants like ours can't grow on the moon because
(a) it is too wet and cold;
(b) there is no air or water;
(c) there are no gardeners.

10 Do you think this is a good description of the moon? Write out a list of things you might want to know about the moon that the passage does not tell you. Then try to find out answers to your questions.

Big Fat Rosie

Big Fat Rosie was the biggest, fattest person
there ever was.
She was bigger than a barrel.
She was plumper than a pudding.
5 She was rounder than a rubber ball.
And almost as heavy as a medium-sized
hippopotamus.
And Big Fat Rosie was very, very wide. She
was so wide that:
10 She had to sit on an extra-wide chair.
She had to sleep in an extra-wide bed.
She had to eat with an extra-wide spoon.
And all the doors in her house were extra-extra
wide, so that she could move from room to
15 room without getting stuck.
    Everything that Big Fat Rosie did was
done enormously. When she ate (with her
extra-wide spoon), she made a noise like
this

20 When she slept (in her extra-wide bed),
    she snored like this

              and all the walls quivered.
        When she cried, like this,

such huge tears fell from her eyes that
25 everything around her became soaking wet.

Turnip Tom and Big Fat Rosie
Mary Calvert

1 Which things were made especially for Rosie?
2 What else might have to be made especially for her?
3 What happened to the walls when Rosie snored?
4 What do you think the cat did if Rosie started crying?
5 How would the other people at home feel when Rosie started to snore?
6 What might happen to Rosie in other people's houses?
7 What did Rosie use for eating with?
8 Write these three headings in your book. Add other words to the lists that could describe Rosie.

bigger than   *plumper than*   *rounder than*
a barrel   a pudding   a rubber ball

9 Why did everything get wet when Rosie started crying?
10 Make up some sound words of your own for eating, snoring and crying.

A companion for Dino

It's a great surprise for everyone when another dinosaur is found in the old chalk pit. This one will be company for the one they found before.

Fancy finding another dinosaur hibernating in the old chalk-pit — a companion for Dino! Jed Watkins couldn't get over it. Using two cranes and slings, workmen had managed to lift this colossal animal out
5 of the layer of fine sandstone in which it had lain for millions and millions and millions of years. Jed had immediately named this animal "Sauro".

Jed looked round at his father, warden of the village recreation ground, who was standing among the crowd
10 of villagers.

"Look, Father!" he shouted, his voice shrill with excitement. "Sauro is smaller than Dino, but I bet you could drive a tractor between his bandy legs without actually touching him."

15 "A small tractor, perhaps," Mr Watkins agreed, smiling.

Sauro, warming up by a bonfire, shook himself and rose slowly to his feet. Dino moved forward and Sauro seemed delighted to see him. Their great long necks
20 swayed to and fro above the crowd and they prodded each other with their small snake-like heads. The sudden noise of aircraft flying low overhead did not disturb Dino, but Sauro raised his head and probed the air at this unknown danger. His muscles rippled under
25 the hide and his tail twitched nervously.

"Will he be all right, sir?" asked Jed anxiously,

turning to Mr Holloway, his headmaster.

"Oh, yes, yes, I'm sure he'll soon settle down. Animals are just like people. They don't take to change
30 at first. Give him time. Remember a modern world must be a confusing and frightening place for a dinosaur."

Two Village Dinosaurs
Phyllis Arkle

1 How did Sauro warm up?
2 Which dinosaur was the bigger?
3 What was Jed's father's job?
4 What was found in the old chalk pit?
5 How did the workmen get Sauro out of the pit?
6 What did the dinosaurs do when they met?
7 Why was Dino not disturbed at the sound of the aircraft?
8 What three things tell you that Sauro was nervous?
9 In what way does the passage say that animals are like people?
10 Find out and write down the meaning of these words in the passage.

crane (line 3)   colossal (line 4)
fine (line 5)   confusing (line 3)
warden (line 8)   hide (line 25)
change (line 29)   prodded (line 20)

Run, Monkey, run

Here is a passage with some words missed out. Read the passage first. When you have read it, write the words you think should go in the spaces.

Small Monkey sat in a tree.

The tree was near the houses, on the edge of town.

Small Monkey looked . . .1. . . through the branches.

He could see a white gate, and a path, and . . .2. . . flowers, and green grass. Some days, a little boy came along the . . .3. . . and threw a nice tit-bit to Small Monkey; an apple-core or a . . .4. . . of chocolate, or, best of all, a sugar lump.

Small . . .5. . . sat in the tree and waited for the little boy . . .6. . . come. All the hot afternoon he waited. The shadows moved . . .7. . . the grass. Small Monkey felt so hungry; but the . . .8. . . boy did not come. No one came. They were all asleep, in their . . .9. . . in the hot afternoon.

Small Monkey . . .10. . . a little to himself, and said he would go home. Just then, quick . . .11. . . tap-tapped along the footpath. Small Monkey saw a . . .12. . . woman in a white dress, with a basket on her . . .13. . . She stopped at the gate, opened it, and . . .14. . . towards the house. "Yoo-hoo! Lucy! Are you there?"

Small Monkey Tales
John Cuncliffe

Discuss the words you chose with your friends.

Noah and the ark

Now do the same for this passage.

Inside the ark Noah and his family waited and listened, . . .1. . . nothing happened that day, nor the next, nor the next. Seven days Noah and . . .2. . . family waited and listened, then . . .3. . . heard it. Splat, splatter, splash. Rain fell . . .4. . . the ark. It rained harder and Noah looked . . .5. . . through the window. He saw angry clouds and lightning. He heard the thunder . . .6. . . and the wind roar.

The animals . . .7. . . frightened, but Noah and his family . . .8. . . God would take care of . . .9. . . .

The water . . .10. . . deeper and deeper. The ark was . . .11. . . on the waves, but it had been . . .12. . . well and rode safely . . .13. . . the storm.

One day Noah felt the bottom of the ark . . .14. . . the ground. Noah sent . . .15. . . the black raven and the white dove, but they . . .16. . . returned to the ark. Noah said the water is . . .17. . . covering the trees. Then one day the dove . . .18. . . back an olive leaf, and another day she didn't . . .19. . . back at all.

Days and days went . . .20. . . . Noah and his family looked out and saw . . .21. . . the ark was resting high up in the mountains. They saw trees that . . .22. . . uprooted, but the ground . . .23. . . dry and the grass was growing. Noah opened the doors . . .24. . . the cages and the animals hurried out.

Noah and his family knelt . . .25. . . and thanked God for keeping them safe.

Dragons

There have been stories about dragons for hundreds and hundreds of years. The stories are about a giant flying animal, like a lizard which often breathes fire.

The name *dragon* comes from a Greek word which
5 means serpent. In pictures some dragons look just like large serpents, others look almost like dinosaurs. This is very strange because the stories about dragons were invented long before anyone knew that dinosaurs had ever lived.

10 We do not know what a dragon is. Many years ago people did not know what animals from far away lands looked like. Men who had been to lands where animals like tigers, leopards and crocodiles lived tried to draw these animals and tell people what they had seen.
15 Often their drawings were not very good and it was hard to tell about them in words. They spoke of cats much larger than a wild cat, with fierce claws that could tear a man to pieces. Or big, scaly animals with long tails and rows of big teeth. They told about giant birds
20 that flew down and carried off lambs. As the stories were told again and again the animals became bigger, their claws sharper and their tails longer. This may be one way in which stories about dragons began.

It's strange how there are many different kinds of
25 dragon. This often seems to depend on the countries the stories came from. Dragons from China usually are friendly and bring good luck. They have no wings but they are able to fly. English dragons are dark, ugly and do wicked deeds. Often they guarded treasure.
30 Sometimes heroes or brave knights came to kill them.

You will know the story of St George, for example. He killed a dragon and rescued a princess.

1 Where does the word *dragon* come from?
2 Which dragons are dark and ugly?
3 What job did English dragons often have?
4 What did St George do?
5 Which animals do dragons look like?
6 What does the passage say about Chinese dragons?
7 Why is it strange that in pictures some dragons look like dinosaurs?
8 Why did people many years ago not know what some animals looked like?
9 What do you think these animals are
  (a) cats much larger than a wild cat;
  (b) big scaly animals with long tails and rows of big teeth;
  (c) giant birds that carry off lambs?
10 Find out what these words mean.

  lizard (line 3)   serpent (line 5)
  invented (line 8)   scaly (line 18)
  guarded (line 29)

11 Write out the words in the passage which tell you what dragons can look like.

Dark is necessary

Plop is a baby Barn Owl. Now, as you know, owls sleep in the daytime and hunt for food at night. But Plop is afraid of the dark and he has a lot of adventures before he comes to know and love the dark.

"Plop!"

"Yes, Mummy?"

"Go and find out some more about the dark, please, dear."

5   "Now?" said Plop.

"Now," said his mother. "Go and ask that little girl what she thinks about it."

"What little girl?"

"That little girl sitting down there — the one with the

10 pony tail."

"Little girls don't have tails."

"This one does. Go on now or you'll miss her."

So Plop shut his eyes, took a deep breath, and fell off his branch.

15 His landing was a little better than usual. He bounced three times and rolled gently towards the little girl's feet.

"Oh! A woolly ball!" cried the little girl.

"Actually I'm a Barn Owl," said the woolly ball.

"An owl? Are you sure?" she said, putting out a

20 grubby finger and prodding Plop's round fluffy tummy.

"Quite sure," said Plop, backing away and drawing himself up tall.

"Well, there's no need to be huffy," said the little girl. "You bounced. You must expect to be mistaken for a

25 ball if you bounce. Do you say 'Tu-whit-a-woo'?"

"No," said Plop. "That's Tawny Owls."

"Oh, you can't be a proper owl, then," said the little girl. "Proper owls say 'Tu-whit-a-woo'!"

"I am a proper owl!" said Plop, getting very cross. "I
30 am a Barn Owl, and Barn Owls go 'Eeek' like that."

"Oh, don't do that!" said the little girl, putting her hands over her ears.

"Well, you shouldn't have made me cross," said Plop. "Anyway – you can't be a proper girl."

35 "What did you say?" said the little girl, taking her hands off her ears.

"I said you're not a proper girl. Girls don't have tails. Squirrels have tails, rabbits have tails, mice . . ."

"This is a pony tail," said the little girl.

40 "But why do you want to look like a pony?".

"Because – oh, because it's the fashion," said the little girl. "Don't you know anything?"

The Owl who was Afraid of the Dark
Jill Tomlinson

1 Read the introduction again. Why does Plop's mummy want him to find out more about the dark?
2 What does the little girl think Plop is, at first?
3 What sounds do Tawny Owls make?
4 How does Plop get from the tree to the little girl's feet? Try not to miss anything out.
5 Why does Plop get cross with the little girl?
6 Why does the little girl put her hands over her ears?
7 What puzzles Plop about the pony tail?
8 Look at the words in this list. Write down the ones you think fit Plop.

clever   cuddly   grown up   curious
wise   soft   skilful   tawny   fluffy   cold

9 What would you tell Plop about the dark?
10 Why do you think Plop is afraid of the dark?

Sharks

A shark is a fish. It lives in water and breathes through gills like all fish.

Sharks do not lay eggs. They give birth to live baby sharks.

There are about 250 different kinds of sharks, some big, some small, some dangerous, some not. Below are some of the things we know about sharks.

Name	Maximum length	Type	
Tiger shark	5.4 metres	A dangerous shark	It will swallow anything that will fit into its mouth. In ten years tiger sharks may use up to as many as 24,000 teeth. It has about 40 or 50 pups at a time. Each is about half a metre long — about the size of a full grown cat. They can swim as soon as they are born and can look after themselves right away.
Great white shark	6.3 metres	The most dangerous of all sharks.	It doesn't usually swim in shallow waters. It can eat creatures half its own size and often attacks other creatures from below.

Name	Maximum length	Type	
Basking shark	10.5 metres	A harmless shark	It has hardly any teeth. The basking shark does not hunt for food. It swims slowly with its mouth open. As water passes through, tiny fish and plants get caught in its gills — like a tea strainer.
Hammerhead shark	3.6 metres	It is a dangerous shark.	It eats smaller sharks. Often it eats sting rays — these have one or two poisonous spines but this doesn't seem to bother the hammerhead.
Whale shark	15 metres	This is the world's biggest shark.	It is bigger than two lorries. It weighs as much as six cars. It will not attack anyone. Swimmers have been known to ride on its back. The whale shark eats small fish and plankton — the tiniest living things in the sea.

1 How does a shark breathe?
2 Which is the most dangerous shark of all?
3 Which sharks are harmless?
4 What do you learn about baby sharks?
5 How does the basking shark get its food?
6 Write down the name of each shark, starting with the smallest and ending with the largest.
7 If you were a sting ray, which shark would you try to keep away from?
8 Why would a basking shark not make a very good hunter?
9 Why would you not be in danger from a great white shark at the seaside?
10 Read the words in this list and write down the words which you think fit the basking shark.

    fierce   dangerous   kind   small
    harmless   large

The garden

Read the passage below. It tells you all about a picture you have to draw and colour. Read all of it first and think about it before you begin to draw your picture. Make sure you don't miss anything out.

It is a sunny day in your picture. The sky is blue with only three white clouds in it. There are no birds in the sky.

In the middle of your picture stands a house. It has a
5 black roof and two small chimneys. There is no smoke coming out of the chimneys, because it is a warm day. There are three windows upstairs in the house, the middle window has yellow curtains and the other two windows have green curtains.
10 Downstairs there is a black door underneath the window with yellow curtains. On either side of the black door are windows with blue curtains. The house has a garden. There is a green lawn and three trees on each side of the house. The garden has many red and
5 yellow flowers. There is a path leading from the door, through the lawn to a white gate.

Beyond the gate is a lane and coming up the lane are two children dressed in jeans and teeshirts. The boy has a big red ball and the girl holds a brown lead which
0 is fastened to a black and white dog. They are going towards the house. They live there.

Excuses, excuses

When Father came home after a very hard day, he found that things had not been very peaceful at home, either. Everything had gone wrong, but it was hard to tell who was to blame.

"This has been a trying day for me, too," said Mother. "All of the children and the dog and the cat have been bad. I scarcely know whom to blame most."

"It was not my fault," said Dora. "Frank struck me
5 with his fist, and to prevent myself from falling down, I held tightly to his hair. Then he cried and said that I had attacked him."

"You should never strike your sister with your fist," said Father to Frank. "Indeed, I am ashamed of you."
10 "It was not my fault," said Frank. "Dora did not tell you everything. I did not strike her until she sat heavily on the ship model I was building. When I complained about that, she pulled my hair."

"You know very well," said Mother, "that Dora sat
15 on your ship model because she stumbled when Emily splashed green paint on her."

"Is that true, Emily?" asked Father.

"It was not my fault," said Emily. "I was quietly painting a picture when the dog put his foot into a jar of
20 green paint and splashed me all over. In my confusion I may have splashed a little paint on Dora, who was laughing so hard that she did not get out of the way."

"For shame, Bonzo!" cried Father to the dog. "You are not fit to be a house pet if you are so clumsy and
25 foolish as that."

Bonzo hung his head and slunk into a corner.
"It was not Bonzo's fault entirely," said Wilhelmina.

The Sorely Trying Day
R. and L. Hoban

1 Why was Father ashamed of (*a*) Frank (*b*) Bonzo?
2 Why was Dora laughing at Emily?
3 What was Frank making?
4 Write these happenings in the correct order.

Dora sat on Frank's model.
Dora pulled Frank's hair.
Dora stumbled when Emily splashed the paint.
Frank hit Dora.
Bonzo put his foot in the paint.

5 Do you think mother was on Dora's side or Frank's, or did she blame them both? What makes you think so?
6 Do you believe that Dora held on to Frank's hair just to stop herself from falling?
7 All the children have an excuse. What might Bonzo's be?
8 What do you think Father said to Mother before she spoke at the start of the passage?
9 What do you think of the children all blaming each other?
10 Choose one of the children's stories and tell it in your own words.

Little old Mrs Pepperpot

There was once an old woman who went to bed at night as old women usually do, and in the morning she woke up as old women usually do. But on this particular morning she found that she had shrunk to
5   the size of a pepperpot, and old women don't usually do that. The odd thing was that her name really was Mrs Pepperpot.

"Well, as I'm now the size of a pepperpot, I shall have to make the best of it," she said to herself, for she
10   had no-one else to talk to. Her husband was out in the fields and all her children were grown up and had gone away.

Now she had a great deal to do that day. First of all she had to clean the house, then there was all the
15   washing which was soaking and waiting to be done and lastly she had to make pancakes for supper.

"I must get out of bed somehow," she thought and taking hold of a corner of the eiderdown she started rolling herself up in it. She rolled and rolled until it was
20   like a huge sausage which fell softly on the floor. Mrs Pepperpot crawled out and she hadn't hurt herself a bit.

The first job was to clean the house, but that was quite easy. She just sat down in front of a mouse hole
25   and squeaked till the mouse came out.

"Clean the house from top to bottom," she said, "Or I'll tell the cat about you." So the mouse cleaned the house from top to bottom.

Little Old Mrs Pepperpot
Alf Proysen

44

1 What happened to Mrs Pepperpot that does not usually happen to old women?

2 How did she get out of bed?

3 Why did she have to talk to herself?

4 What jobs did she have to do?

5 How did she get the mouse to work for her?

6 What do you think her husband's job was?

7 Can you think of any other way she could have got out of bed without hurting herself?

8 How do you think she felt when she found she had shrunk?

9 Write the sentence in the passage that tells you Mrs Pepperpot had a very busy day ahead of her.

10 Talk with your friends to see if you can think of how she might get the washing done and the supper cooked.

Magic moment

A musician called Antonio is making a record in a studio. Other people are watching from the control room working the machinery for making the record.

Antonio played – a stream of sound, grave and gay, sometimes quick and dancing, sometimes quiet. As the minutes ticked by on the control room clock, I began to feel sleepy.

5   I thought my eyes must be playing tricks on me in the pipe smoke. At the edge of the pool of light, at the point where light met dark, I thought I saw something move. I watched. No. I must be imagining. There was nothing.

10   But the thing moved again, flickering, wavering like a cobweb, to and fro. Something was there. Suddenly Bob clutched at my sleeve, pointing.

"Look! Look! D'you see what I see?"

Into the pool of light a tiny figure was advancing.
15   With quick bursts of scurry it moved towards the player – stop, go. Intent on the music, drawn by it as by a thread, a small grey mouse ran and paused and ran again until it was quite close to the figure bent over his instrument. There it stopped and waited. Not hurrying,
20   it stood up on two legs, like a dancer poised for his solo. Slowly it went forward, its short forepaws held out, balancing, swaying to the music, fascinated. We held our breath.

Without warning the playing stopped. The lights
25   were switched on, the magic was switched off. Antonio threw down his guitar and yawned and stretched and lit

46

a cigarette. He had seen nothing. Nothing was there. We had seen what few people could hope to see in a lifetime. Wasn't I lucky!

Here Be Lions
Sybil Marshall

1 What instrument was Antonio playing?
2 Where did the writer first see the movement?
3 What did the mouse look like as it waited?
4 How did the mouse move after Bob saw it?
5 In your own words, write about what the mouse did.
6 Why had Antonio not seen anything?
7 Why, at first, did the writer not believe what she saw?
8 Why do you think the writer began to feel sleepy?
9 Describe Antonio's music in your own words.
10 Do you think the writer was lucky? Why?
11 What do you think it was like in the control room? Write out the best words to describe it.

noisy   hot   stuffy   cool
fresh   smoky   pleasant   quiet

First published in 1982 by
Basil Blackwell Ltd
Reprinted six times

Reprinted in 1992, 1993, 1994 by
Simon & Schuster Education

Reprinted in 1995 by
Stanley Thornes (Publishers) Ltd
Ellenborough House
Wellington Street
CHELTENHAM GL50 1YW
England

96 97 98 99 00/10 9 8 7 6 5 4 3 2

ISBN 0 7487 1995 4

Printed in Hong Kong by Wing King Tong Co. Ltd.

Acknowledgements
We are grateful to the following for permission to reproduce copyright material:
the author for an extract from *Turnip Tom and Big Fat Rosie* by Mary Calvert, published by BBC Publications 1972.
We regret that we have been unable to trace the copyright owner of "Witches' Spells" by A. Nightingale, and would welcome any information that would enable us to do so.